CONTENTS

INTRODUCTION

The dinosaurs are dead. As dead as a packet of frozen peas and they're not coming back. But there is a way that you can see them with your own eyes and find out what they were really like and sniff their smelly breath and even get chased by them. I'm talking about *time travel*...

Now I know that time-travel technology is in its infancy – well, to be honest it hasn't been invented yet. But just imagine if it were possible. And just imagine that top TV presenter Will D Beest and Mickey, his pet monkey, were about to make a time journey back to see the dinos...

I'LL BE GETTING CLOSE TO DEADLY DINOS!

How would they prepare for it?

How would they get on?

What would happen next?

Well, keep imagining because you're imagining the rest of this book. And that's great because as you turn the pages you'll be imagining that you're watching dinos with Will and Mickey. So good luck and remember, whatever you do – DON'T GET EATEN!

HOW TO WATCH DINOS WITHOUT GETTING EATEN FOR LUNCH

Professor N Large, the inventor of the time machine, is showing his invention to Will and Mickey...

In fact the time machine is very easy to operate. All you do is sit in the cubicle and set the time dial to the year you want to visit. In the case of the dinos that year will be a very, very, *very* long time ago because the dinos died out in about 65 million BC. Experts divide the time the dinos lived into three eras...

MYA = MILLION YEARS AGO

NOW

TRIASSIC 251–199 MYA

JURASSIC 199–145.5 MYA

CRETACEOUS 145.5–65.5 MYA

But of course the Professor isn't going to let them whizz back to dino times just like that. For one thing they need to know the basics about dinos, and they need to pack and learn the safety rules. Hmm – come to think about it that's THREE things...

DINO-SPOTTERS' LESSON 1:
DINO BASICS

Here's a dino and one of the dino's closest cousins...

SPOT THE DIFFERENCE COMPETITION

At first sight there aren't too many differences. The dino and the crocodile are both reptiles, both breathe air and have scaly skin and claws and lay waterproof eggs.

But there's one BIG difference – the dino's legs are tucked under its body. And that means it can walk with its legs straight and breathe more easily on the move because its body doesn't swing from side to side.

DINO-SPOTTERS' TRAINING SESSION:
WALK LIKE A DINO

You will need:
A dinosaur (just kidding!). You can experiment on yourself plus a good friend
An area of open space such as a park, garden or school playground

What you do:
1 Get in position.
2 You should try to walk like a crocodile. Your friend walks normally.
3 Try to walk 30 metres.

You should find:
Your friend will have no difficulties – but you'll find it hard to keep up with them and your legs will start to ache.

HORRIBLE HEALTH WARNING!
Don't do this experiment in school assemblies or anywhere where there are bandy-legged teachers who might think you're making fun of them.

This is because:
Like a crocodile, you're trying to walk with your legs sprawled to the sides. You'll find that you have to move one leg at a time and it's quite tiring. Your friend finds it

easy to walk like a human or dinosaur because they are using 50 per cent less energy than you. So dinos were better walkers and runners than other reptiles. And those lovely straight legs proved ideal for supporting bigger and bulkier bodies – which is why the dinos grew so scarily sizeable.

But dinos were more than crocodiles with long legs. Over time some of them changed. Here is a dinosaur called *Avimimus* (ah-vee-mi-mus) and one of its closest cousins.

SPOT THE DIFFERENCE COMPETITION

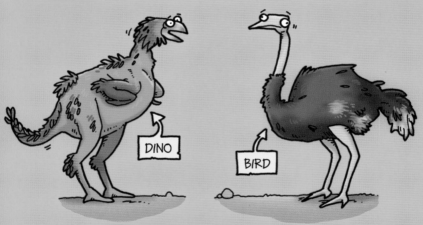

Yes, this dino *does* look like a giant bird. Many dinos had beaks and feathers and scaly legs and their skeletons look similar too. And although no dinosaur could fly, feathers kept small dinos warm, provided some protection from bites and bright colours to attract a mate. So they weren't such a feather-brained idea.

Dinos came in different shapes and sizes – from lethal long-legged lizard look-alikes to fearsome feathered fiends. Will's been writing some notes on the main types to look out for on his time journey...

Will D Beest's dino-spotting notes

Memo

Must remember to check my hair's OK before we start filming.

The main types of dinosaur

Theropods

These dinos walked on two legs and some of them were a bit nippy. Since they were all meat-eaters they might want to nip me too.

Sauropods

The long-tailed, long-necked dinos could grow to horribly huge sizes. I better make sure I don't get under their feet or I might end up as a prehistoric pancake, and that wouldn't be good for my image as a TV star.

Bird-hipped dinos

A very diverse group of dinos as you can see. Luckily, they're all plant—eaters but some of them can be a bit grumpy first thing in the morning so I'd best not mess with these vicious vegetarians.

Bet you never knew!

The bird-hipped dinos got their name because their hipbones look similar to bird hips. Oh, so you've figured that out? Well, I bet you never knew that theropods and sauropods are known as lizard-hipped dinos. And just to confuse you, the birds developed from the lizard-hipped dinos.

Mind you, all this chat about developing dinos raises the very complex and brain-scrambling question of how animals change. Well, this'll take a bit of imagining...

Picture a herd of plant-eating dinos. They're all the same type of animal but some are bigger than others and some are a bit browner. Now imagine a drought that drags on for years and years. Most plants die and turn brown, and after a few years the dinos that are still around are smaller because they can survive on less food and browner because they can hide better from hungry meat-eaters. It's called evolution and it happens all the time. The dinos were around for 165 million years so they had plenty of time to evolve into lots of different shapes and sizes.

DINO-SPOTTERS' TRAINING TEST:
DESIGN A DINO

Imagine you're a mad scientist planning to invent new kinds of dinos. Which qualities would be useful for a meat-eater and which would suit a plant-eater?

a) Small, fast-moving body
b) Big, strong body
c) Armour and spikes
d) A big brainy brain
e) Big sharp teeth and claws
f) Singing ability

Meat- and plant-eating dinos really did evolve like this. But no dino needed a brainy brain or an ability to sing, which is why the dinos never got to read *Horrible Science* books or invent pop music. Mind you, the dinos' puny brains were perfectly suited to their way of life and smart enough to eat you.

You'll notice that being an evolving dino is an either/or business. For example, a plant-eater can't be armoured and a fast-runner because the armour would be too heavy, and a running meat-eater can't be too big or it would be too heavy to run very far. This makes the dino-design rules fairly straightforward.

DINO–DESIGN RULES FOR MAD SCIENTISTS.

BIG MEAT–EATERS EAT BIG PLANT–EATERS PLUS ARMOURED PLANT–EATERS IF THEY'RE FEELING LUCKY.

SMALL SPEEDY MEAT–EATERS EAT SMALL SPEEDY PLANT–EATERS

CRUNCH

DO YOU MIND? I'M EATING!

So there are the dino basics and Will and Mickey can't wait to tear off to the Triassic and peek at their prehistoric pals. But the Prof reminds them that there were no supermarkets in prehistoric times and they'll need to take everything they need. Which is quite a polite way of telling them to *get packing*!

DINO-SPOTTERS' LESSON 2:
GET PACKING!

Will and Mickey sit down and write out detailed lists of things to take – that way they'll leave nothing vital behind.

List of things I'll need for dino-watching
by Will D Beest

Time Machine
(this is VITAL)

Map, compass and weather forecast

Peanut butter and jam sandwiches and thermos

Sleeping bag in case I have to spend the night.

First-aid kit

Sunscreen

Notebook and pencils

High-powered binoculars

Camera and spare batteries (I wouldn't want to miss a great picture of myself and a dino!)

Rucksack to put it all in.

LIST OF THINGS
I'LL NEED FOR
DINO-WATCHING
by Mickey
1 One large bunch of bananas
2 Nuts for nibbling

Clothes are very important (well, they are for humans – Mickey will be wearing his normal monkey skin). Unfortunately Will has chosen some really unsuitable clothes for dino-watching...

HOW DO I LOOK?

PONG

AFTERSHAVE FOR THAT TOUCH OF ELEGANCE.

HORRIBLE HAWAIIAN SHIRT. THOSE BRIGHT COLOURS ARE SURE TO FRIGHTEN OFF DINOS ONCE THEY'VE STOPPED LAUGHING.

NO! NO! NO!

TRENDY BAGGY SHORTS AND FLIP-FLOP SANDALS TO STAY COOL. OK – SO MAYBE THEY WOULD HAVE BEEN TRENDY IN THE AGE OF THE DINOS.

Will's sandals are useless for walking distances and his shorts leave his legs exposed to scratches and insect bites. Small dinos could do terrible things to his knees. That shirt won't really scare a dino although it's sure to scare anyone with good taste. Scientists think that dinos had excellent colour vision and a hungry meat-eater would spot Will a mile off. As for the aftershave – meat-eaters had a good sense of smell and one whiff of Will and they'd have been after him.

So the Professor orders Will to change into something more sensible.

BETTER?

NO AFTERSHAVE
OR SCENTED SOAP
ON SKIN

CAMOUFLAGE CLOTHING
TO BLEND IN WITH THE
SURROUNDINGS

THICK TROUSERS
TO PROTECT LEGS

STURDY
WALKING
BOOTS

Oh well, at least Will got the hat right first time. It's ideal for shading him from the sun and keeping his head dry in the rain. And now for the all-important safety rules.

DINO-SPOTTERS' LESSON 3:
HOW <u>NOT</u> TO GET EATEN

THE FIRST AND BEST ADVICE FOR ANY UNTRAINED DINO WATCHER IS BEWARE! DINOSAURS CAN BE VERY DANGEROUS INDEED.

Even the big plant-eaters that spend their lives peacefully trashing trees can trample you flat if you go too close to their babies. And as for the meat-eaters … well, I'm not going to tell you what the Prof told Will and Mickey. If I did you'd probably be too scared to turn the page and your teeth would chatter so loud that they'd fall out.

But don't let the danger put you off – dino-watching can be incredibly exciting and incredibly interesting just so long as you do it SAFELY. And staying safe means being prepared. The Professor is talking Will and Mickey through these vital safety rules...

YOU CAN'T MONKEY AROUND WITH THESE!

1. DON'T FEED THE DINOSAURS. They might decide to feed on you!

2. NEVER GO DINO-WATCHING ON YOUR OWN. And always leave a note to say where you've gone.

3. NEVER TRY TO GET CLOSE TO ANY DINO. It's safer to watch them from a safe distance without them seeing you.

4. KEEP AWAY FROM DANGER AREAS. These include...

• Dinosaur nesting areas - mother dinos may try to defend their nests.

• Dead dinos - meat-eaters may come to feed on the body.

• Waterholes in dry areas - a meat-eater might be lurking in ambush.

5. NEVER TAKE ANY SMELLY FOOD OR COOKED MEAT TO EAT. The meat-eating dinos will sniff you out.

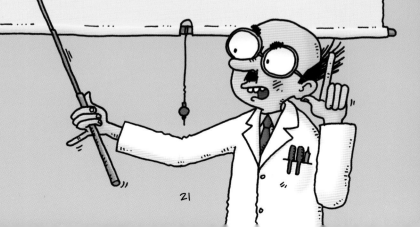

6. TAKE CARE WHEN WATCHING A HERD OF PLANT-EATING DINOS. The males may want to defend their females and the females may want to defend their babies.

7. ALWAYS HIDE YOUR TIME MACHINE SOMEWHERE SAFE AND DON'T WANDER TOO FAR AWAY. You may need it in a hurry.

8. IN AN EMERGENCY YOU MIGHT BE ABLE TO CLIMB A TREE. But beware, some small meat-eating dinos live in trees.

9. DON'T LEAVE ANYTHING OR TAKE ANYTHING FROM THE DINOSAUR'S WORLD. Taking things is especially dangerous as it might cause a malfunction of your time machine and strand you in hyperspace for a few million years.

10. WATCH OUT FOR VOLCANOES! In the dino era there were many more volcanoes than nowadays. Avoid them - especially if they're just about to explode!

GOOD LUCK! (You're going to need it!)

Of course the dinosaurs are really very dangerous. (Did someone just say that?) So the Professor is recommending the following optional safety equipment...

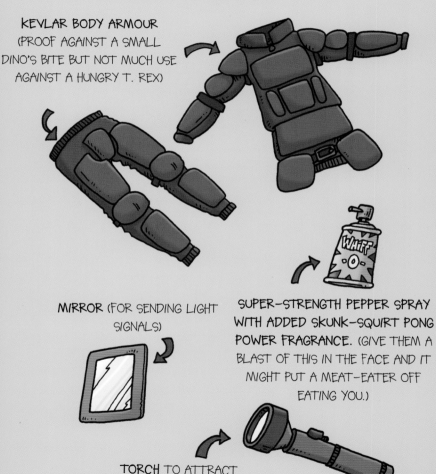

KEVLAR BODY ARMOUR
(PROOF AGAINST A SMALL DINO'S BITE BUT NOT MUCH USE AGAINST A HUNGRY T. REX)

MIRROR (FOR SENDING LIGHT SIGNALS)

SUPER-STRENGTH PEPPER SPRAY WITH ADDED SKUNK-SQUIRT PONG POWER FRAGRANCE. (GIVE THEM A BLAST OF THIS IN THE FACE AND IT MIGHT PUT A MEAT-EATER OFF EATING YOU.)

WHIFF

TORCH TO ATTRACT ATTENTION IF YOU GET LOST

A final question...

With that final warning ringing in their ears Will and Mickey set off on their first time-trek.

THE TERRIBLE TRIASSIC

Sorry, readers! In the previous chapter I forgot to show you Will and Mickey's map and weather forecast. Here's their map of the world 200 mya...

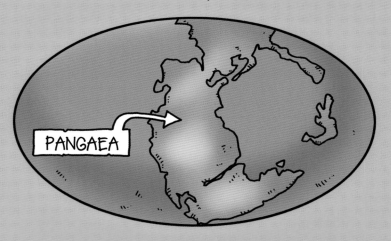

PANGAEA

You might wonder why all the continents are muddled up and clumped together. Well, it's all to do with hot rocks.

Although it's hard to imagine, the ground is actually a vast slab of rock floating on a sea of hot melted rock 100 km under your backside. (It's lucky this rock is so thick – any thinner and you might suffer from a badly burnt bottom.)

These slabs of rock are known as "plates" – which is odd as they don't break and you wouldn't want to eat your dinner off them. Over time they jostle together and some plates move under or over each other or move apart and molten rock wells up to fill the gap.

As the plates scrape past each other they trigger earthquakes and volcanoes. There are seven big plates and lots of smaller ones, and although they move slower than your hair growing (16 cm a year) – over millions of years they do get around. In the past 200 million years – a single great island called Pangaea has split apart to make the continents we know today. Now let's check out the weather…

Triassic weather forecast
Today will be pleasantly warm and mostly dry – especially in the centre of Pangaea, which is mostly desert. There will be no snow anywhere on Earth – not even at the north and south poles – so you can forget about skiing. The outlook is for more of the same for the next 40 million years, and it's going to get even hotter and drier so make sure you take an extra bottle of water and some wet-wipes.

The Triassic sounds a great place to chill out on the beach, but Will and Mickey will have to beware of swimming. The seas around Pangaea are full of savage swimming reptiles, although none of them are dinosaurs. The reptiles include turtles, nothosaurs (no-tho-sores) and ichthyosaurs (ick-thee-oh-sores).

TURTLE

NOTHOSAUR

ICHTHYOSAUR

The reptiles share the seas with new kinds of coral and some shockingly savage-looking sharks.

At last Will and Mickey are ready to set off on their time trip. The journey to the Triassic is fast and silent, and they're there before they know it. The first thing Will and Mickey notice when they step out of their time machine is that there isn't any grass or flowers.

WILL'S DINO SAFARI

THE ONLY TREES ARE PRIMITIVE PINES AND MONKEY PUZZLES.

TRIASSIC PINE TREE

MONKEY-PUZZLE TREE

PUZZLED MONKEY

WHY DO THEY CALL THEM "MONKEY PUZZLES"?

AH THAT'S THE PUZZLE...

THERE ARE PLENTY OF COCKROACHES, TERMITES AND DRAGONFLIES.

FLYING REPTILES CALLED PTEROSAURS HAVE EVOLVED. AND OH YES...

THE ANCIENT RELATIVES OF CROCODILES.

TO BE CONTINUED

As you've just seen there are various bugs and croc-like creatures and flying reptiles about in the Triassic. Here are some more Triassic beasts that weren't dinos that Will and Mickey might bump into … if they're unlucky.

Name: **POSTOSUCHUS**
(post-oh-sook-us)
Size: Up to 6 metres long
Lived: 222-215 mya
Location: USA (that's to say the land now known as the USA — I expect the dinos called it something else. The modern place name will be given for all locations in this book.)
Spotters' notes: These ruthless reptiles are the biggest meat-eaters in the late-Triassic and every plant-eater's worst nightmare. Their dagger-like teeth and fast-moving legs make them creatures to avoid, so dino-spotters beware.

Name: **CYNODONT**
(sign-oh-dont)
Size: Up to 1.5 metres long
Lived: 222-215 mya
Location: Arizona, USA
Spotters' notes: Cynodonts are "mammal-like reptiles" –that's to say reptiles that are evolving into mammals. Cruel Cyno is hairy like a mammal but lays eggs like a reptile. It lives in burrows and has a horrible habit of eating its young when it gets peckish, although it normally scoffs roots and small animals.

And here are some of the main types of dinos that you might spot. I ought to warn dino-spotters not to expect to see too many dinos in the Triassic because they were still fairly rare for most of the era.

DINO-SPOTTERS' GUIDE TO TRIASSIC DINOSAURS

Name: **EORAPTOR**
(ee-oo-rap-tor)
Size: 1 metre long
Lived : 230-225 mya
Location: Argentina
Spotters' notes: This small and nimble dino is one of the first to evolve. It's actually an early theropod and dino-spotters should check out its unusual five-fingered hand although only the three clawed fingers were of any use. Unusually for a meat-eater, Eoraptor munched vegetables too so you might glimpse it lunching on leaves.

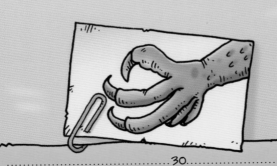

Name:

HERRERASAURUS
(he-ray-ra-sore-us)
Size: 4 metres long
Lived: 230-225 mya
Location: Argentina
Spotters' notes: Herrerasaurus is another early dino.

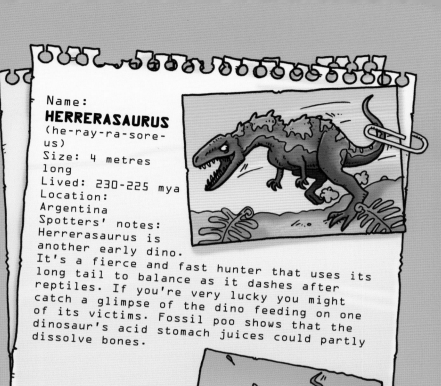

It's a fierce and fast hunter that uses its long tail to balance as it dashes after reptiles. If you're very lucky you might catch a glimpse of the dino feeding on one of its victims. Fossil poo shows that the dinosaur's acid stomach juices could partly dissolve bones.

HONK

PONG

Name: **PLATEOSAURUS**
(plat-ee-oh-sore-us)
Size: 6-10 metres long
Lived: 216-219 mya
Location: All over Pangaea
Spotters' notes:
With its long neck and tail Plateosaurus looks like a sauropod ... but it's not. It's a prosauropod - part of a group of early plant-eaters that has nothing to do with the later giants.

It's easy to tell the difference — unlike a sauropod, Plat plods on its hind legs. But although it's a peaceful plant-chomper those eyes on the sides of its head will soon spot you if you get too close, and it might try to fight you off with its fearsome thumb spike. And you wouldn't want to thumb a lift from this grumpy greenery guzzler, now would you?

Name: **COELOPHYSIS**
(seel-oh-fy-sis)
Size: 2.8 metres long
Lived: 215-210 mya
Location: North America
Spotters' notes: These small but deadly dinos have three sharp claws on each hand and 100 sharp teeth, and they scrunch anything they can sink their jaws into. Worse still, they hang out in packs so you might see lots of them all trying to grab a share of you.

Having shaken off the ancient version of crocs, Will and Mickey are still exploring the Triassic...

WILL'S DINO SAFARI

THIS CUTE LITTLE COELOPHYSIS BABY WON'T HARM US.

TUG

WHAT ABOUT THE NOT-SO-CUTE COELOPHYSIS DADDY?

Bet you never knew!

"Cute" isn't the word you instantly think of in connection with dinos. But otherwise normal dino-spotters have been known to go gooey over baby dinos. Maybe those big eyes and big heads remind us of human babies? Some dino experts reckon adult dinos react in the same way and that's why they don't absent-mindedly gobble their babies for breakfast. Well, not that often, anyway.

Oh dear – it looks like Will and Mickey missed out on spotting a vital clue that every dino-spotter needs to know about – that fresh dino dung close to the *Coelophysis* baby… An expert could have told them which dino made it and when.

DINO-SPOTTERS' LESSON 4:
DINO DUNG

Take a long close look at this dino dung. Go on, you know you want to…

A large poo generally comes from a larger dino and a squelchy warm wet poo comes from a dino that visited the spot not long ago. So if you find a giant warm wet meat-eater's poo it's time to GET OUT OR GET ATE!

By the end of the Triassic era the dinos were getting bigger and greedier, and their long legs made them speedier than other reptiles. But they weren't the top beasts by any means – well, not until right at the end of the Triassic when something NASTY happened – a mass extinction. (That's when loads of life forms suddenly die off.)

The Triassic mass extinction may have been triggered by volcanic eruptions. Experts think the gruesome gas from the volcanoes changed the climate suddenly and many of the big reptiles were bumped off. In all, half of all the life forms on Earth were wiped out. But the dinosaurs did rather well out of it. With most of their reptile rivals out of the way, they were ready to rule the Earth.

THE GIANT JURASSIC

The phrase "bigger and better" might have been invented for the Jurassic – the era when dinos got even bigger and better at killing each other. Will and Mickey have managed to escape back to their time machine and now they're zooming through hyperspace to the Jurassic.

By the start of the Jurassic the world is a very different place to back in the hey-day of the Triassic. Just compare this map to the one on page 25.

Pangaea is busy splitting into two giant islands – Gondwana in the south and Laurasia in the north. Ultimately the dinosaurs in the two islands will evolve differently, but in the early days there are land bridges that the dinos can cross.

At the seaside, life is just as dangerous. The nasty nothosaurs have died out but the ichthyosaurs are still swimming around, and they've been joined by plesiosaurs (pleez-ee-oh-sores). The pitiless plesiosaurs scrunch super-sized sharks and feast on fish and squid-like things called belemnites (bell-em-nites). Meanwhile the mammal-like reptiles are down but not quite out. And there are still a few hair-ing – I mean *haring* – around in the Jurassic. Here's one now...

Name: **CASTROCAUDA**
(cas-tro-cord-a)
Size: 43 cm long
Lived: 164 mya
Location: China
Spotters' notes:
Crazy-looking Cas looks like a cross between a beaver and a duck-billed platypus. It burrows in riverbanks and spends its life scrunching fish.

Meanwhile the genuine mammals are evolving, but they stay sensibly small and hidden away in burrows and out of sight of the deadly dinos. The mammals only creep out at night when the dinosaurs are having a dino-snore.

At the same time the weather is changing. As seas widen the air gets wetter and that means rain.

Jurassic weather forecast

You'll need your waterproofs for the next 66 million years because it's going to be wet. There will be heavy rain in most coastal areas and there are flood warnings for low-lying and swampy areas. The weather will stay warm in all parts with few traces of snow or ice even at the poles. There will also be long sunny spells and dry weather in desert areas.

With a lurch and squelch, Will and Mickey's time machine arrives in the Jurassic and lands in a huge muddy puddle. It looks like they're in a jungle. All this rain means that the typical Jurassic greenery is lusher and bigger than in the Triassic. There are plenty of cycads, gingkoes and tree ferns. The ground is covered in horsetails and they can see huge conifer and sequoia forests on the drier hills.

The warm wet weather is good news for bugs. Alongside the cockroaches, dragonflies and termites there are now ants and beetles (and some beetles are happily munching dino dung). Will is just photographing the bugs when Mickey points out something very exciting...

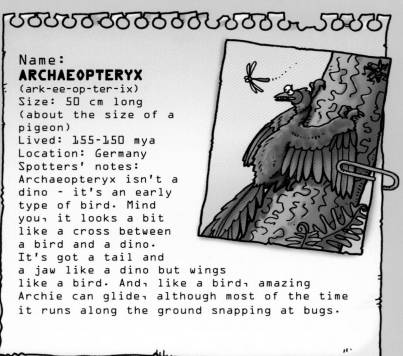

Name:
ARCHAEOPTERYX
(ark-ee-op-ter-ix)
Size: 50 cm long
(about the size of a
pigeon)
Lived: 155-150 mya
Location: Germany
Spotters' notes:
Archaeopteryx isn't a
dino - it's an early
type of bird. Mind
you, it looks a bit
like a cross between
a bird and a dino.
It's got a tail and
a jaw like a dino but wings
like a bird. And, like a bird, amazing
Archie can glide, although most of the time
it runs along the ground snapping at bugs.

For millions of years the pterosaurs have been the only sizeable creatures in the air – but now they've got rivals. Dino experts aren't sure how the birds evolved – but they probably started off as small, feathered theropod dinosaurs. Will is so excited by the *Archaeopteryx* that he almost misses the line of footprints in the mud. Dino tracks. Time to try out another set of vital dino-spotters' skills...

DINO-SPOTTERS' LESSON 4:
TERRIBLE TRACKS

Here's some dino tracks to look out for on a dino-spotting trek...

Deeper tracks are made by heavier dinos and more widely spaced dino tracks were made by running dinos. A few tracks show dinos getting up to other things...

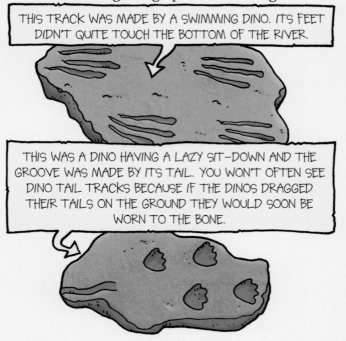

THIS TRACK WAS MADE BY A SWIMMING DINO. ITS FEET DIDN'T QUITE TOUCH THE BOTTOM OF THE RIVER.

THIS WAS A DINO HAVING A LAZY SIT-DOWN AND THE GROOVE WAS MADE BY ITS TAIL. YOU WON'T OFTEN SEE DINO TAIL TRACKS BECAUSE IF THE DINOS DRAGGED THEIR TAILS ON THE GROUND THEY WOULD SOON BE WORN TO THE BONE.

DINO-SPOTTERS' TRAINING SESSION:
MEASURE A DINO TRACK

Once you start your time-trek you'll be able to do this for real. But for the moment you can practice with a good friend.

You will need:
A good friend
A tape measure
A piece of soft ground or wet sandy beach (but there's no need to start squelching about in a smelly swamp)

What you do:
1 Ask your good friend to walk on the soft ground.
2 Carefully measure the length of their footprint.
3 Next measure the length of their outside leg from the ground to their hip bone.

You should find:
Their leg should be about 3.5 to 4 times the length of their footprint. I said "about" because some people have very large feet and short legs. But it's roughly right for humans and dinos too. So if you find some dino tracks you can get a rough idea of how tall the dino was.

DINO-SPOTTERS' TRAINING TEST:
COULD YOU BE A DINO-TRACKER?

All you need to do is select the answers to the questions – but you're not allowed to time-trek back to the Jurassic to check your answers!

1 Sauropods had claws on their back feet. Why?
a) For defence.
b) So they wouldn't slide down slippery slopes.

2 Scientists have found dinosaur tracks leading up a cliff. What's the explanation?
a) Some dinos were excellent climbers.
b) The rock had tilted upwards over time.

3 How could sauropods walk on their toes when their bodies were so heavy?
a) They wore high heels.
b) They could only move one leg at a time.

HIGH HEELS ARE SO LAST CENTURY!

Meanwhile, back in the Jurassic, Will and Mickey are still following the dino footprints they discovered...

WILL'S DINO SAFARI

Is Will about to be swallowed by the smelly swamp? Will Mickey flee to the tree or hop the twig? Whilst we're waiting to find out, here's some more about awful Al and other dangerous dinos from the giant Jurassic.

DINO-SPOTTERS' GUIDE TO JURASSIC DINOSAURS

Name: **ALLOSAURUS**
(Al-o-sore-us)
Size: Scary - 15
metres long
Lived: 150-135 mya
Location: USA
Spotters' notes:
Awful Al is every
sauropod's worst
nightmare - well,
that's assuming you
can have nightmares
with a brain the
size of an apple.
Al's the only dino
that can scrunch a
sauropod, and it
enjoys scrunching the odd
Stegosaurus too. If you see a herd of
plant-eaters - beware. Despite its huge
size, Al likes to lie low. It will
charge the petrified plant-eaters and
choose the weakest victim, stabbing it
with its knife-like lower teeth and
ripping off a huge hunk of flesh.

Name:

STEGOSAURUS
(steg-oh-sore-us)
Size: 9 metres
long
Lived: 155-145 mya
Location: North
America
Spotters' notes:
Stupid Steg ambles
at about 6-8 km
per hour with a
brain the size of
a walnut, but

maybe that's why dino-spotters are
fond of Steg. After all it makes us
look super-brainy. But stegosaurs are
more lethal than they look. It's true
that the plates on their back are
useless for defence, but the spiked
tail is a dangerous weapon. And that
means any dino-spotter who gets too
close to a mother Steg and her babies
must be a bit of a walnut-brain too.

Name: APATOSAURUS
(a-pat-oh-sore-us)
Size: 21 metres long
Lived: 161-145 mya
Location: North
America
Spotters' notes:
Dino-spotters are
sure to spot a few
sauropods such as
Appy lumbering
along in a herd or
pausing to munch
trees or slurp on
swampy vegetation.

And if you don't see any, you'll hear
their ear-splitting farts. Sauropod guts
contain bacteria that help digest their
dino dinners. These microbe mates rot
the tonne of greenery that Appy chomps
every day just to keep its huge body
going. Although Appy has no armour, its
huge size makes it hard to attack, and a
whack from its tail can break every bone
in your body so keep
clear of them.

Name: **BRACHIOSAURUS**
(brak-ee-oh-sore-us)
Size: 23 metres long
Lived: 155-140 mya
Location: North America
and Africa
Spotters' notes:

Even Brach's forelegs
are taller than a man
and its huge neck is
nine metres long. As
you'll see, even though
the Brachiosaurus likes
to munch leaves from
trees it can't raise
its neck very far
above horizontal even
when it sits back and
takes the weight on its tail. If you're
lucky you might see Brach gulping
boulders to help it grind the food in
its gut (its teeth are used for raking
in leaves). When the boulders are too
smooth to be useful the dino will sick
them up — so beware of low-flying
burped-up boulders.

GAG

Name:
COMPSOGNATHUS
(comp-sog-nath-us)
Size: 70 cm long
(mostly tail)
Lived: 145 mya
Location: Europe
Spotters' notes:
This hen-sized dino
spends its time
snapping after
insects and
lizards. It's not

much of a fighter as each hand only has
two claws but it's good at hiding so
you'll probably only spot it when it
steals your sandwiches or bites your
backside. For scientists, the interesting
thing about this scaled-down dino is how
similar it is to Archaeopteryx. The two
beasts lived at the same time and in the
same place, and some of Compy's Chinese
relatives even had feathers like a bird.

Name: **DILOPHOSAURUS**
(di-loaf-oh-sore-us)
Size: 7 metres long
Lived: 190 mya
Location: USA and China
Spotters' notes:
Dangerous Dilo is a
dandified dino with a
crazy crest to impress
lady dinos. The teeth
on this fashionable
flesh-feaster look evil
enough, but the real
danger comes from its
cruel claws. The
flexible thumb joint
allows the deadly dino
to grasp small reptiles and mammals and
rip them to bits. The jaws are just
strong enough to chomp the body bits.

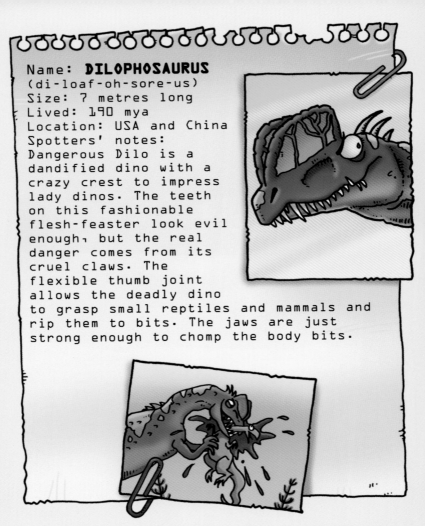

But talking about being chomped to body bits let's find
out what's happening to Will and Mickey...

WILL'S DINO SAFARI

Will and Mickey have crawled out of the swamp but angry Al is waiting.

Al's arms are too short to prevent the horrible hunter crashing over when it trips, and broken ribs were a common result. Doesn't your heart go out to the poor darling? Well, the deadly dino will have your heart out if it catches you!

BEASTLY BABIES

Will and Mickey have survived their potentially lethal trip to the Jurassic. And now they're off to the Cretaceous. Will they ever learn? As soon as they step out of their time machine they're nearly knocked sideways by a low-flying plane ... well, actually it's one of these...

Name: **QUETZALCOATLUS**
(ket-zol-co-at-lus)
Size: 1.8 metre-long body, 11-metre wingspan
Lived: 84-65 mya
Location: North America
Spotters' notes: This phenomenal pterosaur is one of the largest flying animals ever. It usually feasts on fish but it won't turn its enormous beak up at a nice smelly dead dino. It spends most of its time soaring above lakes in search of a likely lunch.

A nearby volcano blowing its top has startled the terrible pterosaur. But antisocial volcanoes are part of life in the Cretaceous, as Will and Mickey's weather forecast makes clear...

The weather is set to stay generally mild and there will be warm and cool seasons known as "summer" and "winter". There will be frequent volcanic eruptions with lots of ash falls, smelly gases and acid rain.

The cause of all these evil eruptions are massive movements of the plates. The islands of Gondwana and Laurasia are slowly cracking apart and the continents we know today are appearing – as you can see for yourself in Will and Mickey's map.

Once again a seaside swim is off-limits. The ichthyosaurs are on the way out, but the plesiosaurs have been joined by the mosasaurs (moze-ah-sores). These toothy terrors grow to over 17 metres and gobble fish, turtles and you if you happen to take a dip at the wrong moment. But talking about badly timed dips – riverbanks are haunted by a giant crocodile with a nasty habit of chomping any creature that comes close.

Name:
SARCOSUCHUS
(sar-co-soo-cus)
Size: 11-12 metres long (that's four times the size of a modern croc)
Lived: 110 mya
Location: Niger, Africa

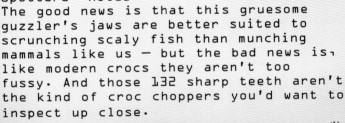

Spotters' notes: The good news is that this gruesome guzzler's jaws are better suited to scrunching scaly fish than munching mammals like us — but the bad news is, like modern crocs they aren't too fussy. And those 132 sharp teeth aren't the kind of croc choppers you'd want to inspect up close.

Will and Mickey start to explore. They soon spot a few birds and one of the birds spots Will with a splat of poop on his head. The feathered flappers of the Cretaceous look a bit different from today's winged wonders – many have claws on their wings, for example. But there's one type of animal that they don't see. Most of the mammals are still keeping a low profile in their burrows. Never mind – our dino-spotting duo soon stumble across something even more amazing...

It's a *Maiasaura* (my-ah-sore-ah) nesting site. *Maiasaura* are 9-metre-long plant-eating dinosaurs – the name means "good mother lizard" – and Will and Mickey are about to find out how good they are...

WILL'S DINO SAFARI

TO BE CONTINUED

Silly Will! Maybe he should have read his own notes about dino eggs and nests...

Will D Beest's Dino-spotting notes

Eggs and nests

Sauropods and most meat-eaters lay their eggs in sheltered places and leave them, but other dinosaurs build nests. Dinos such as Maiasaura and Orodromeus (or-oh-dro-me-us) nest in groups and the adults look out for attackers. The adult dinos often defend their nests and youngsters so it's a good idea to avoid these sites or the adults might get over egg-cited.

MUMMY!!

Although the adults can often see off an attacker, smaller sneaky nest raiders can help themselves to baby dinos...

If you're ever silly enough to get close to a dino's nest I bet you'll be amazed by how small the eggs are compared to an adult dino. There's a reason why most eggs are smaller than footballs and it's not that the dinos liked a kickabout. The developing dinos breathe through the eggshell. But if the egg was too big the shell would be too thick for the poor little baby dino to breathe.

Of course the fairly small size of the eggs does create a problem for a dino mum who wants to keep them warm. I mean she can't exactly sit on them. Why? Because she would have invented the omelette 65 million years early and the dinos would have ended up getting egg-stinked, I mean extinct. But some dinos have hit on a way to keep their eggs warm without splatting them...

DINO-SPOTTERS' TRAINING SESSION:
BUILD A DINO NEST

You will need:

A spade or trowel

At least six egg-shaped pebbles (you could use ordinary eggs but ask permission to use them first otherwise you'll have to "shell out" for new ones)

Some leaves or grass clippings

Gloves

Tape measure

An open piece of earth in a safe place such as your garden, school grounds or a sandy beach

HORRIBLE HEALTH WARNING!
You won't get away with digging up your dad's prize-winning pumpkin patch so don't try or you might share the fate of the dinos.

What you do:

1 Don't forget to bandage any cuts on your hands and slip on your gloves before handling any germ-infested soil.

2 Make a nest shape like this

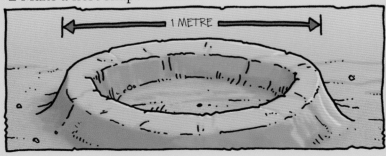

1 METRE

If the soil is really dry and dusty you could sprinkle it with a little water to make it firmer.

3 Line the nest with leaves or grass clippings.

4 Lay the pebbles or eggs in a circle in the nest.

5 Cover the eggs with some more plant material and sprinkle some soil or sand on top of them.

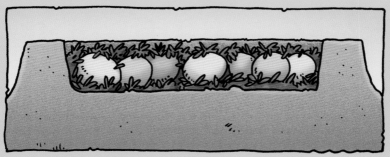

You should find:

CONGRATULATIONS – you've built a nest similar to an *Orodromeus* or *Maiasaura* nest but half the size. The plant material isn't just there to cushion the fragile eggs. The plan is that it will rot and produce heat – birds called scrub fowl use this technique to warm their nests today. And that means the dinos invented central heating!

MMM... TOASTY!

Once the dinos have hatched they mostly wander off and have to feed themselves, but baby *Maiasaura* get fed by their parents until they're big enough to leave the nest. It's hard to imagine the dinos feeding their little ones, but just picture your mum sicking Brussels sprout soup down your throat and you'll get the idea. (On second thoughts forget I ever said that.)

Bet you never knew!
To reach the size of an adult Maiasaura, the babies need to get 16,000 times bigger. If you'd been growing this fast you'd weigh as much as a herd of elephants. That's an awful lot of slimy sprout soup.

ANY CHANCE OF A ROLL WITH MY SOUP, MUMMY?

CRUEL AND CRAZY CRETACEOUS DINOS

Maiasaura are amazing enough, but as Cretaceous dinos go, they're fairly normal. They don't look weird and they don't have outrageously cruel habits. Will and Mickey are on the lookout for some even more awesome dinos. Something like this little lot...

DINO-SPOTTERS' GUIDE TO CRETACEOUS DINOS

Name: **OVIRAPTOR**
(oh-vee-rap-tor)
Size: 1.8 metres long
Lived: 85-75 mya
Location: Mongolia
Spotters' notes:
If you happen to speak Latin you'll know that this dino's name means ''egg thief'' - which is silly because it doesn't steal eggs (there's no egg-scuse for this). Instead the oddball Oviraptor crushes shellfish in its beak like a giant parrot. Mind you, it's not clever to go up to it and start squawking, ''Who's a pretty oviraptor?''

CRUNCH

Bet you never knew!

Ovi wasn't as odd as its relative Incisivosaurus (in-si-siv-oh-sore-us) that lived in China 120 mya. Unlike Ovi this feathered dino had teeth, including a pair of giant gnawing teeth at the front of its mouth. It looked like a cross between a road runner and a big goofy bunny.

WHO-TH GOOTHY LOOKING?

Name: **THERIZINOSAURUS**
(ther-i-zine-oh-sore-us)
Size: 9.6 metres long
Lived: 70 mya
Location: Mongolia, China, North America
Spotters' notes: Crazy dinos don't come weirder than this curious creature. The giant claws look scary but this feathered plant-eater spends its life feeding its gigantic gut. In fact it's probably the world's laziest dino, and the creepy claws are just there to strip the leaves off trees and scare away any meat-eater that fancies a Therizinosaurus for tea.

Name: PARASAUROLOPHUS
(pa-ra-sore-rol-of-us)
Size: Up to 10 metres long
Lived: 76-74 mya
Location: Canada
Spotters' notes:
Pointy-headed Para belongs to a big group of plant-eating dinos called hadrosaurs that amble across North America towards the end of the Cretaceous. Hadrosaurs generally walk on their hind legs and have hundreds of grinding teeth for pulping tough plants. If you imagine a herd of vegetable blenders you'll get the idea. Anyway, what makes Para a bit special is the way it sounds. That tube on its head is a natural wind instrument, and by puffing up it the dino makes a deep note. It's ideal for attracting attention or warning of an attacker. The noise travels over a wide distance but is surprisingly hard to pin-point. I bet it'll drive you mad as you try to spot the dino.

Name:

TRICERATOPS

(try-sera-tops)
Size: up to 9
metres long
Lived: 67-65 mya
Location: North
America
Spotters' notes:
The full Latin name
of this awesome
animal means "scary
three-horned face"

although its mum probably loves it. The
horns are as dangerous as they look and if
you want to know what this pushy plant-eater
is like just imagine a rhinoceros with an
attitude problem. If it's attacked, a
Triceratops herd will form a circle around
their young but an adult Triceratops might
decide to charge you (so you'd better be
able to run at 20 km per hour to get away
from it).

Name: EUOPLOCEPHALUS
(you-oh-plo-kef-ah-lus)
Size: 6.5 metres long
Lived: 76 mya
Location: North America
Spotters' notes:
Elephant-sized Euo looks a bit like a tank on four legs. The whole of its back and head and even its ugly

eyelids are covered in bony armour. But Euo has a weakness - there's no armour on its tummy so if you have superhuman strength you can flip it over. That's what T. rex tries to do but Euo has a 20-kg club on its tail. Can you imagine trying to flip a six-tonne oil drum? It's a tough task, especially when the oil drum is trying to smash your knees with a sledgehammer. When it's not nobbling T. rex, Euo spends its day peacefully munching juicy plants and digging up roots.

Name: **TROODON**
(troh-oh-don)
Size: 2.4 metres
long
Lived: 75-70 mya
Location: North
America
Spotters' notes:
Talented Troodon is
the all-time dino
brain-box champ. Not
that there's much
competition, and
Troodon is just a
budgie-brain in a
ruthless reptile body. Dino-spotters may
have a tough time finding Troodon
because this dino spends its time
hiding. It's most active at dusk and
dawn when its large forward-facing eyes
are suited to hunting small mammals and
birds. Amongst its other dirty deeds
thieving Troodon likes to lay its eggs
in other dino's nests to make the other
dense dinos look after its yucky
youngsters.

Name: VELOCIRAPTOR
(vel-oss-ee-rap-tor)
Size: 3 metres long
Lived: 67 mya
Location: Mongolia
Spotters' notes:
It's fast, it's
feathered and it's
fearsome. Vicious
Velo looks like a
cross between a
bird and a dino,
but in fact it's
100 per cent dino
and 101 per cent
deadly. It likes to
leap on its victims
and use its scary
second toe as a grisly
grappling hook. To make things even
scarier, Velos hunt in packs and they
have excellent sight and smell. So the
best advice is to keep your distance
and then some more. And you might like
to know that there's a whole grisly
group of feathered raptors with similar
loathsome lifestyles such as the bigger
and even more murderous Deinonychus
(die-no-ny-kus).

Name: **TYRANNOSAURUS REX**
(ty-ran-oh-sore-
us recks)
Size: 12 metres
long
Lived: 67-65 mya
Location: North
America
Spotters' notes:
Every dino-
spotter wants to
see a T. rex but
this could be the
last thing you

ever see. T. rex has sharp eyesight and a good sense of smell, and to make matters worse bacteria between the monster's dagger-like teeth make wounds go bad and give the dino a deadly bite — and just as deadly bad breath. Safety armour and a super-strength anti-dino spray are vital — but they aren't enough. A T. rex can crush a car with one bite and gulp down half a human in a single gargantuan greedy gobble. Most T. rexes hunt alone but they can live in small groups. But life with the rexes can be tough — they sometimes fight and kill each other and guzzle other T. rexes' babies.

HE LOOKS LIKE A
TASTY SNACK!

Bet you never knew!

Other parts of the world have T. rex-style dinos too — for example Giganotosaurus (gig-an-oh-toe-sore-us), a deadly dino that lived in Argentina 93-89 mya, is even bigger than big bad T.

The problem with writing a dino-spotters' guide to the Cretaceous is that there's not enough space to cover the dizzying diversity of dinos — especially the crazy ones. So I've put them in a quiz instead...

DINO-SPOTTERS' TRAINING TEST:
SPOT THE DODGY DINO
Which of these crazy Cretaceous dinos are real reptiles and which are just too dodgy to be true?

1 This **STYGIMOLOCH** (stij–i–mol–ock) has a huge lump on its head and sharp teeth – even though it's a plant-eater.

2 If you're stupid enough to kiss a **MASIAKASAURUS** (mah–si–a–ka–sore–us) you'll get a gobful of razor-sharp teeth.

3 Scientists claim the newly discovered **SUBMARINOSAURUS** (sub–ma–rine–oh–sore–us) is more than a strong swimmer. Its fish–like gills actually allow it to breathe underwater.

4 LOOK OUT BELOW! This four-winged **MICRORAPTOR** (my-cro-rap-tor) dino can glide from the trees and land on your head.

5 This mean-looking **CARNOTAURUS** (car-no-tore-us) has horns like a bull but it's not as cuddly.

6 MULTILIMBOSAURUS (mul-ti-lim-bo-sore-us) has no shortage of legs. The dino can even survive when a T. rex bites a leg off.

Answers:

Real reptiles

1 Scary *Stygimoloch* lived in the USA 70 mya. The 3-metre dino might have used its bony bonce to bash other male dinos at breeding time.

2 Murderous Maz lived in what's now Madagascar 67 mya. This 6-metre-long toothy terror stabbed small animals before shredding them. It needed a good dentist if you ask me.

4 Experts reckon that the feathers on this tiny 39-cm-long dino allowed it to glide. It lived in China 126 mya.

5 Cruel Car lived in Argentina 115 mya. The 7.5-metre dino had horns to impress female dinos but they weren't much use in a fight. Mind you, these sharp teeth could grab a bite and make a plant-eater feel that something was missing from its life – like its leg.

Dodgy dinos

3 Dinos could swim and some ate fish but they certainly couldn't breathe underwater.

6 No dino had more than four limbs.

It's nearly the end of the Cretaceous and one thing seems sure. The dinos are on a roll – there are loads of them in all shapes and sizes, and it looks like they're here forever. But then something goes horribly, dino-crunchingly wrong – what is it? Will and Mickey had better beware. It might CRASH on top of them!

THE DINOS' DAY OF DOOM

It would take a very brave time traveller to go back to the day the dinos met their doom to find out what happened to them. If the time traveller wasn't brave they could be incredibly stupid instead, and that brings us to Will D Beest...

WILL'S DINO SAFARI

HOW FASCINATING. A PACK OF YOUNG T. REXES. THEY'RE HUNGRY BECAUSE THEY NEED TO PUT ON 2 KG A DAY.

WELL, I'M NOT FOR TEA – REX!

TO BE CONTINUED

Has time run out for Will and Mickey? All will be revealed, but first this chapter's supposed to be about how dinos died out, so let's check out what happened to them...

PICTURE THE SCENE...

It's a Sunday afternoon 65 million years ago. The plant-eating dinos are contentedly guzzling the greenery and letting out loud happy farts of contentment. Meanwhile the meat-eaters are snoozing off a hearty great dead-dino dinner.

Suddenly something eyeball-bustingly bright rips across the sky followed by a blastwave throwing trees about like twigs and turning entire forests into sheets of white-hot flames. It's die-now time for the dinos, and if they had any brains they'd know that life would never be the same again. Well, to be more exact, they aren't going to have much more life.

OK – so I made up the bit about Sunday afternoon but the rest might really have happened. An asteroid – that's a huge lump of space rock – smashed into the Earth with the force of billions of atom bombs.

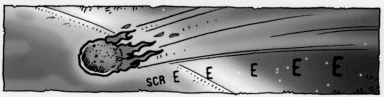

Some dinos were blasted by the impact, which centred on Yucatan, Central America.

Some dinos were cooked by forest fires caused by the heat of the blast.

The blast sent huge amounts of sulphur into the air. It formed acid rain which dissolved dino flesh.

The ash blotted out the sun for years and most plants died. The plant-eaters starved. Then the meat-eaters starved because there weren't enough plant-eaters to scrunch.

The creatures that coped best were burrowing beasts and small creatures that could hide from the devastation. In the seas the ammonites, belemnites and giant reptiles kicked the bucket (well, they would have done if buckets had been invented but they hadn't so they just croaked instead). The pterosaurs got in a flap and flopped, but the birds survived by the skin of their beaks.

The problem for the dinos after the asteroid blast was that they were too big and too hungry to survive in a world where there wasn't much food. Even the smaller dinos couldn't cope with the tough times and that's why all that remains of the dinos are a few fascinating fossils.

DINO-SPOTTERS' LESSON 6:
HOW TO BE A FOSSIL FREAK

As every self-respecting dino-spotter knows, a fossil is a physical trace of an ancient life form. In the case of the dinos that might mean a bone, but it could be anything they left behind...

All these fossils, even the gruesome ones, are clues to a dino's lifestyle, and that's what makes them so fascinating to scientists.

A DINO EGG

A PILE OF DINO POO

SO... HEA—VY!

A SET OF DINO FOOTPRINTS

DINO-SPOTTERS' TRAINING TEST:
COULD YOU BE A FOSSIL EXPERT?

1 What's "pyrite disease"?
a) A deadly disease caught from fossils that slowly turns scientists into living statues.
b) It's when fossils crumble into grey powder.

2 A "headless wonder" is a fossil-hunter's name for a dino found without a head. But why are some dinos headless wonders?
a) Their heads fell off when the dino bodies rotted.
b) Meat-eating dinos enjoyed biting the heads off plant-eaters.

3 Why are some fossils poisonous?
a) The dino was poisoned by a volcano and the body is still dangerous.
b) The poison dripped into the rock containing the fossils.

THUD

Dino bones can turn up in some horribly odd places. For example, there's half an *Apatosaurus* holding up a bridge at a place called Bigelow Brook in the USA. In Wyoming, there's a place called Bone Cabin Quarry named after a hut built out of dinosaur bones. And in the 1890s US fossil finder John Bell Hatcher found dino bones in a monastery in Argentina. No one knows what the fossils were doing there, but they were found next to a collection of pickled human hearts.

PACK YOUR SPARE PANTS, MONSTER BOY. WE'RE OFF TO ARGENTINA!

Mind you, all this talk about fossils raises one tricky but surprisingly fascinating question – how is a fossil made? Well, the most important thing is that the dino's body or whatever it is gets buried in sand, mud or ash very fast.

If it lies around it will rot or get worn away by the weather. Once it's buried, over time the sand, mud or ash gets squashed into rock. Water trickles through the rock and things get very interesting.

Usually the bones rot away, just leaving a hole. Minerals dissolved in the water fill the hole and make a cast (or copy) of the original – in the best fossils the copy is so detailed that dino experts can study microscopic details such as blood vessels.

DINO-SPOTTERS' TRAINING SESSION:
MAKE A FOSSIL

You will need:
PVA (white) glue
Modelling clay or Blu-tack
Rolling pin
Newspaper
A shallow seashell (try saying that with a mouthful of mussels)

What you do:
1 Put down the newspaper – this experiment is MESSY.
2 Roll the clay until it's fairly flat and about 2 cm thick.

3 Press the top of the shell into the clay to make an impression on it.

4 Carefully pour the PVA glue into the impression and leave it to dry. This will take AGES. In the meantime clear up your mess or your mum will make an impression on you ... with the rolling pin.

You should find:
The dried PVA glue has made a cast of the shell. As you've just found out, some fossils are made in the same fashion.

Of course life would be dead easy if scientists could find fossils lying about with neat little signs saying what they were. But often science isn't that nice. Most fossils are scattered amid tonnes of very hard rock found in the hottest, coldest, wettest, driest, loneliest corners of the world. Let's go and join *Horrible Science* dino expert Doug Deeper in Patagonia, South America...

REMOVING A DINO SKELETON CAN TAKE MONTHS OF WORK. WE USE PNEUMATIC DRILLS TO CLEAR THE ROCK ENCASING THE FOSSILS.

Back at the lab, the hard work of removing the fragile fossils from the rock has only just begun. It takes months or even years and involves lots of blasting the fossils with tiny pellets in something called a shot-blasting chamber. It's fun if you like that kind of thing.

But clearing up the bones is just part of the job. If it's a new kind of dino, the bones need to be very carefully drawn and described so scientists will know if they find the same kind of dino again. And then someone needs to think up a nifty name for the new dino. Dino names are Latin or Greek and have two parts (this book mostly lists the first part). The first part is the genus or group of dinos it belongs to. The second part is the species or type of dino it is – so the genus of a *Tyrannosaurus rex* is *Tyrannosaurus* and the species is *rex*.

Some dino names describe what the dino was like, others record the place where it was found or the name of its discoverer. And some dino names are just plain weird.

FIVE WEIRD DINO NAMES YOUR TEACHER WILL PROBABLY THINK YOU MADE UP

1 *Micropachycephalosaurus* (my-cro-packy-cefalo-sore-us) means "small thick-headed lizard".

2 The name *Stygimoloch* (remember that dino from page 70?) actually means "demon from the River Styx" (that's the ancient Greek River of Death).

3 The Australian dino *Atlascopcosaurus* (atlas-cop-co-sore-us) was named after a company that supplied the scientists with drilling equipment.

4 *Leaellynasaura* (lea-elly-na-sore-ra) was named after the daughter of the couple that discovered it.

5 *Bambiraptor* (bam-bee-rap-tor) was named after ... well, some people say it's named after the baby deer in the famous Disney film. But if you try to cuddle this Bambi you might need a new set of fingers.

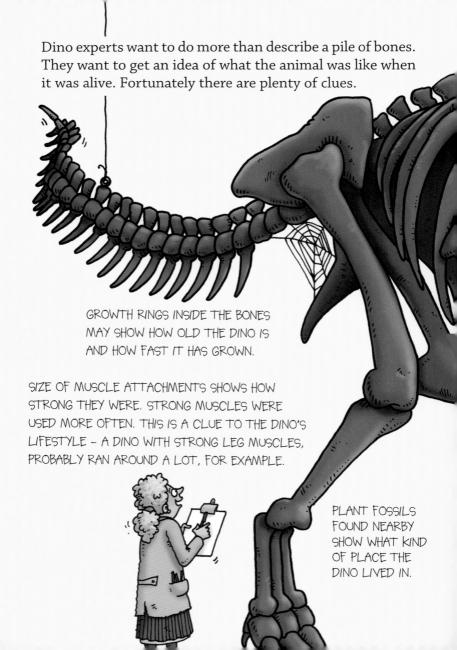

Dino experts want to do more than describe a pile of bones. They want to get an idea of what the animal was like when it was alive. Fortunately there are plenty of clues.

GROWTH RINGS INSIDE THE BONES MAY SHOW HOW OLD THE DINO IS AND HOW FAST IT HAS GROWN.

SIZE OF MUSCLE ATTACHMENTS SHOWS HOW STRONG THEY WERE. STRONG MUSCLES WERE USED MORE OFTEN. THIS IS A CLUE TO THE DINO'S LIFESTYLE – A DINO WITH STRONG LEG MUSCLES, PROBABLY RAN AROUND A LOT, FOR EXAMPLE.

PLANT FOSSILS FOUND NEARBY SHOW WHAT KIND OF PLACE THE DINO LIVED IN.

DINO BRAINS DON'T SURVIVE BUT SCIENTISTS CAN MAKE A CAST OF THE EMPTY BRAIN CASE TO SHOW THE SHAPE AND SIZE OF THE BRAIN.

POSITION AND SIZE OF EYES SHOW HOW GOOD THE DINO'S EYESIGHT WAS.

TEETH, STOMACH CONTENTS AND POO ALL SHOW WHAT THE DINO ATE.

And in all these ways scientists can get a good picture of what living dinos were like. It's the next best thing to bringing them back to life. But talking about bringing back dinos – what *did* happen to Will and Mickey? Well, they've been chased into their time machine by a teenage T. rex. The terrible tearaway wants to tear away a bit of Will. Meanwhile, back at Professor N Large's lab...

WILL'S DINO SAFARI

Good grief – those teeth. Oh well, at least Will "nose" a few things about these ruthless reptiles and you'll be grinning from earhole to earhole to read that Doug Deeper plonked the scaly scaled-down snapper in the time machine and sent it whizzing back to the Cretaceous era.

Hmm – maybe that's the best place for it. What do you think?

Epilogue:
SPOT THE BIRDIE

This has been a guide to dino-spotting, but now you've read this book and imagined what real dinosaurs were like – you might feel sad that they're not around today...

Well, cheer up right now!

It's true that the dinosaurs were awesome to look at and awesomely fascinating but you really wouldn't want them being awesome anywhere near you. After all, the dinos were awesomely good at killing and they were faster and stronger than us. And if the dinos were still prowling our planet no mammal could ever have grown big enough to take them on. We wouldn't have had the chance to evolve into the brainy beings we are today, and we'd all probably look like your hamster.

But that's not quite the end of the dino story. Come to think of it, some dinos *did* survive. In fact it's possible that there could be a dino or two in your garden right now. I'm talking about the small, feathered, clawed, beaky dino descendants known as "birds". Scientists have found so many similarities between birds and dinos that some experts say birds *are* dinos.

So maybe you don't need a time machine to spot a few dinos – just a good imagination!

HORRIBLE INDEX